SERVING IN THE AIR FORCE

Alix Wood

PowerKiDS press.

New York

Published in 2014 by Rosen Publishing
29 East 21st Street, New York, NY 10010

Editor for Alix Wood Books: Eloise Macgregor
Designer: Alix Wood
Researcher: Kevin Wood
Military Consultant: Group Captain MF Baker MA RAF (Retd)
Educational Consultant: Amanda Baker BEd (Hons) PGCDL

Photo Credits: Cover, 1, 4, 5, 6, 7, 8, 9, 10, 11,12,13,14,15 top and
bottom,16,19, 20, 21, 22, 23, 24, 25, 26, 27 middle and bottom, 28, 29, 30
© Defenseimagery.mil; 15 middle © Christopher Halloran/Shutterstock, 17 top
© goretexguy;17 middle and bottom © Shutterstock; 18 © Micha Klootwijk/
Shutterstock, 27 top © Paul Drabot/Shutterstock

Library of Congress Cataloging-in-Publication Data

Wood, Alix.
 Serving in the Air Force / by Alix Wood.
    p. cm. — (Protecting our country)
Includes index.
ISBN 978-1-4777-1297-9 (library binding) — ISBN 978-1-4777-1400-3 (pbk.) —
ISBN 978-1-4777-1401-0 (6-pack)
1. United States. Air Force—Juvenile literature. I. Title.
UG633.W645 2014
358.40023'73—dc23
                              2012043395

Manufactured in the United States of America

CPSIA Compliance Information: Batch #S13PK3: For Further Information contact Rosen Publishing, New York, New York at 1-800-237-9932

Contents

What Does the Air Force Do?

The armed services are made up of highly skilled and trained men and women who defend our country. The US Air Force protects our country by defending the sky over our heads. It is responsible for air warfare and the **bombardment** of other countries in times of war.

There are many different skills needed by people serving in the air force. Pilots fly the aircraft. **Navigators** advise the pilots where to fly. **Technicians** and engineers keep the equipment in good order. Support staff, bomb disposal experts, doctors, chaplains, firefighters, and many other personnel are all essential for the smooth running of the service.

Every job is vital. No one will be flying anywhere if there's a hole in the runway!

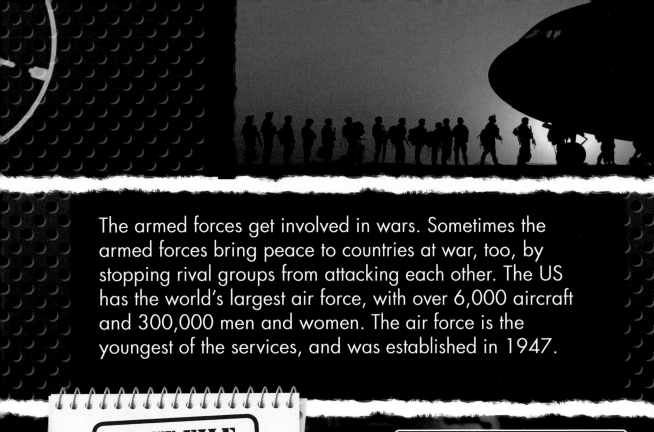

The armed forces get involved in wars. Sometimes the armed forces bring peace to countries at war, too, by stopping rival groups from attacking each other. The US has the world's largest air force, with over 6,000 aircraft and 300,000 men and women. The air force is the youngest of the services, and was established in 1947.

This is the lower deck of a B-52 Stratofortress bomber. The B-52 has been in active service with the US Air Force since 1955.

Fighter Pilots

Fighter pilots face danger each time they go on a mission. There is no second place in aerial combat. You must be better at flying and fighting than your rival, or you risk being shot down.

An F-16's clear **canopy** allows the pilot to see all around. The F-16 can fly very long distances. It can fly over 500 miles (800 km) to attack its target and return to base. F-16s have special equipment on board which lets people on the ground see what the pilots can see, and direct them accurately to a target.

F-16 pilots get great views while flying.

The A-10 Thunderbolt (right) is nicknamed the Warthog. It has an on-board cannon that can fire up to 70 rounds per second! In this picture, the Warthog pilot is firing a flare. The heat from this flare draws enemy heat-seeking missiles away from the aircraft.

Cannon

Flare

FACT FILE

It takes about four years to train as a fighter pilot. You must be physically fit and have excellent eyesight. You must also have good coordination skills. Only the best will become fighter pilots.

G-forces put strain on a pilot's body when flying at top speed. "G" stands for gravity, which pulls objects toward Earth. Normal gravity is 1g. A fighter pilot can reach over 6g. At 6g, the pilot will seem six times heavier, find it hard to breathe, and may black out. Training, **oxygen**, and special "pressure pants" which stop the blood from pooling in the legs all help to fight this danger.

Keeping Them Flying

One of the most important people in the life of a jet fighter pilot is the crew chief. The crew chief is the **mechanic** in charge of making sure that the plane is safe and ready to fly at a moment's notice. The safety of the pilot is in his hands.

The crew chief knows the aircraft from nose to tail. He'll get up about four hours before the plane is due to fly and inspect it for flight. The crew chief **refuels** it, changes the tires, makes sure all the various systems are serviced, hooks up the power, and checks all the instruments and lighting. It is common for a pilot to thank the crew chief every time he or she takes off.

This pilot, in the cockpit of an A-10 Thunderbolt II, relies on his crew chief to keep him safe.

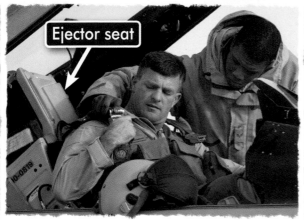
Ejector seat

It is the crew chief's job to check that the pilot is strapped into his ejection seat securely. An ejection seat can save the life of a pilot if the plane is in difficulty.

To eject, the pilot pulls a lever under his seat and the canopy above is blown away. Then the seat is shot out of the plane powered by small rockets. A parachute in the seat will then open.

Canopy

Pilot

This Thunderbird pilot ejected during an air show. He landed safely.

Spy Planes: The U-2

Spy planes fly very high so they cannot be seen. The pilot's job is to take photographs and spy on the enemy. This is called **reconnaissance**. A U-2 can fly day and night, at up to 70,000 feet (21,336 m).

A U-2 above the clouds

The special shape that lets the plane fly so high also makes it very difficult to take off and land. The wings are 130 feet (40 m) from tip to tip and **flex** a little. The pilot's helmet limits his vision, too. Another U-2 pilot has to follow behind in a fast car when the plane takes off. He tells the pilot by radio how close to the ground the wings are.

A U-2 taking off, with a support car following behind.

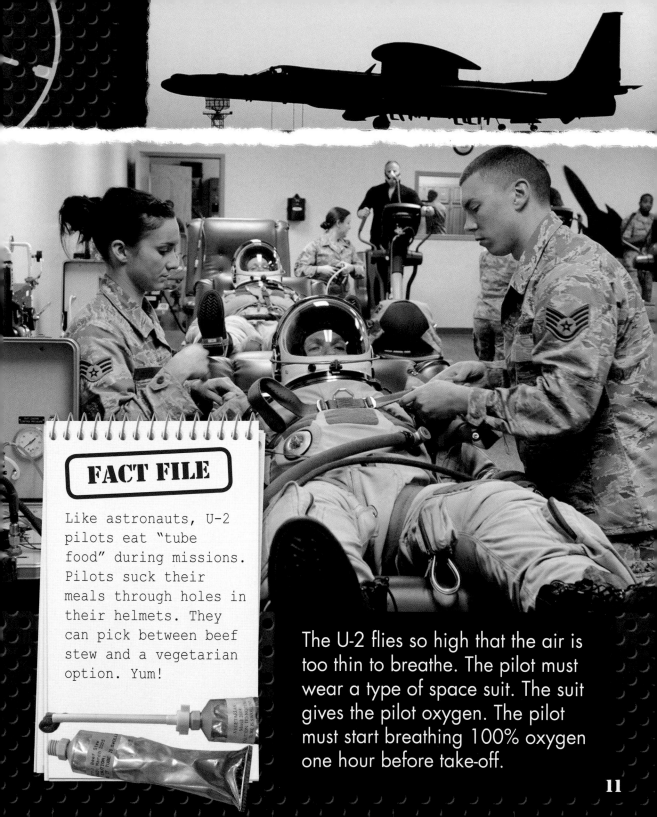

Like astronauts, U-2 pilots eat "tube food" during missions. Pilots suck their meals through holes in their helmets. They can pick between beef stew and a vegetarian option. Yum!

The U-2 flies so high that the air is too thin to breathe. The pilot must wear a type of space suit. The suit gives the pilot oxygen. The pilot must start breathing 100% oxygen one hour before take-off.

Gas Station in the Sky

Sometimes a mission is just too far for an aircraft to fly on one tank of fuel. What if there is nowhere to stop and fill up? What you need is a flying gas station.

Some aircraft's main job is to refuel other aircraft. That's what KC-10s and KC-135s do. Mid-air refuelling helps the other aircraft fly farther, or carry heavier loads than usual. There are two ways to connect to the fuel tanks of another aircraft. You can use either a boom or a drogue. Both are tricky to get right. A boom is a long metal pipe, which a boom operator on the refuelling aircraft moves into position into the aircraft that needs fuel. A drogue is a hose with a basket on the end. The other aircraft puts a probe into the hose to get the fuel.

Boom

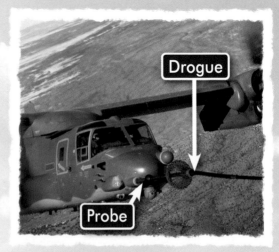
Drogue
Probe

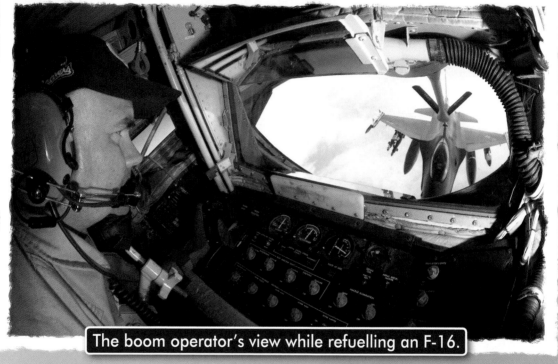
The boom operator's view while refuelling an F-16.

A KC-10 crew has a pilot, co-pilot, flight engineer, and boom operator. The boom operator controls the refuelling. He sits at the rear of the aircraft and looks through a window. He positions the boom with a control stick and gives commands to the other aircraft. Connecting two flying aircraft safely is a very difficult job.

V.I.P. Transportation

The air force also takes care of the aircraft that the President of the United States uses. This is called Air Force One. It is usually one of two specially outfitted Boeing 747s. They are each as tall as a six-story building and as long as a city block. They can travel at 630 miles per hour (1,014 km/h) and can fly halfway around the world on a tank of fuel.

President Obama aboard Air Force One

The flying Oval Office has 4,000 square feet (372 sq m) of floor space on three levels. It has a meeting room, rooms for the president and the first lady, an office for senior staff, another office that can become a medical operating theater, work and rest areas for the president's staff, media, and air force crews, and two kitchens that can feed 100 people at a time! A doctor is also always on board.

FACT FILE

Air Force One is the call sign of any air force aircraft carrying the President. No matter where in the world the President travels, if he flies in an air force jet, the plane is called Air Force One.

Air Force One has the most up-to-date communications. This means that the aircraft can be a flying command center if necessary. Several cargo planes usually fly ahead of Air Force One to provide the President with services he will need in remote locations.

Here, Air Force One flies over Mount Rushmore, which has sculptures of former presidents George Washington, Thomas Jefferson, Theodore Roosevelt, and Abraham Lincoln.

Invisible Aircraft

How do you hide a large aircraft? The US Air Force has developed clever ways to keep some aircraft from being seen in flight. The F-117 Nighthawk, the B-2 Spirit, the F-22 Raptor, and the F-35 Lightning II all use stealth technology to hide from **radar**.

The strange-looking B-2 (below) has a wing shape that makes it almost invisible to radar. The B-2 is made from **carbon-fiber** materials which don't reflect radar well. It has a special coating which reduces the reflection even more. The B-2 injects chemicals into its exhaust fumes to stop any vapor trail, too.

A B-2's see-through vapor trail

Engine

A radar antenna sends out bursts of radio energy, which bounce back from objects they hit. The rounded metal body of a normal airplane reflects radar signals back to the radar. The radar antenna measures the time it takes for the reflection to arrive, and with that information can tell how far away the plane is. Stealth aircraft are shaped so that radar signals are reflected away from the radar equipment.

The position of the B-2's engines on top of its wings, rather than under them, helps make the aircraft hard to spot using **infrared** heat sensors. The wings help hide the heat coming from the engines. A slit-shaped exhaust pipe spreads the hot exhaust fumes, too.

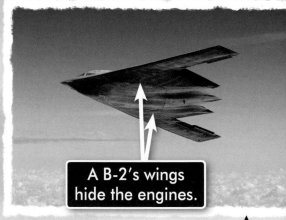

A B-2's wings hide the engines.

A Watcher in the Skies

When you are protecting the skies, it is important to know who is flying around. The air force uses sophisticated radar to spot enemy aircraft. This radar can assess enemy action and keep track of the location of any friendly aircraft in range.

A system called AWACS, which stands for "airborne warning and control system," is mounted onto the back of an E-3 Sentry which is an adapted Boeing 707. The radar can detect, track, and identify low-flying aircraft and sea traffic. It can work in any weather over any terrain. The aircraft's flight crew usually has two pilots, a navigator, and a flight engineer.

Radar

The radar dome is 30 feet (9 m) across and six feet (2 m) thick at the center. It is held 11 feet (3 m) above the aircraft by two struts. It is tilted down 6° at the front to reduce drag during takeoff. The radar spins round six times a minute when it is working.

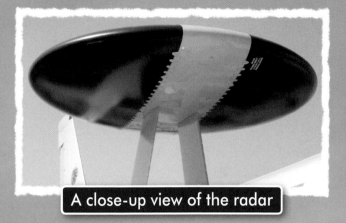

A close-up view of the radar

FACT FILE

In addition to the flight crew, a mission crew of 13 to 19 people is also on board. The crews can work in shifts if necessary and there are on-board areas for rest and eating. The equipment is arranged in bays with different areas for each specialty, such as communications or target identification systems.

Here, mission crew members work at their stations inside an E-3 Sentry.

Firefighting

Air force fire protection specialists (nicknamed fire dawgs) have to deal with fire hazards from burning rocket fuel to brush fires. It can be a dangerous job.

When the Forest Service needs help putting out large fires, the air force's MAFF unit will sometimes come to its aid. "MAFF" stands for "modular airborne firefighting system." The system fits inside a C-130 aircraft. When dropped, its 3,000-gallon (11,356-l) load covers an area a quarter of a mile (0.4 km) long and 60 feet (18 m) wide.

FACT FILE

MAFF units drop either water or slurry. Slurry is water with red coloring and a thickening agent, called ammonium sulfate, added to it. The red color helps pilots see where they have dropped previous loads. Slurry also has fertilizer in it to help the area regrow.

A C-130 drops slurry through a tube in the left rear door of the aircraft.

Firefighters provide 24/7 fire and crash rescue coverage and are organized, equipped, and trained to respond to any emergency. It's a job that demands courage, fitness, and strength. Firefighters deal with dangerous situations such as plane crashes, cleaning up hazardous materials, confined-space rescues, and fuel fires.

These firefighters are wearing aluminized fire protection suits to extinguish a runway fire.

Moving Cargo

The air force is responsible for transporting all kinds of cargo. The loadmaster's job is to make sure that everything arrives safely, whether the cargo is a helicopter, food supplies, or a sick baby. The loadmaster must precisely balance the cargo so the airplane can fly safely.

The loadmaster organises parachute drops of supplies, equipment, and people, too. It's a big responsibility. He needs to check all the equipment. He even pushes the cargo out of the hold while the plane is flying.

An all-terrain vehicle strapped down on a C-17 Globemaster.

A loadmaster pushes water supplies out over Afghanistan.

Equipment must be securely tied down. If a large item moves, it could endanger the aircraft, damage other cargo, and hurt passengers.

Transport aircraft may not seem as exciting as jet fighters or stealth bombers, but they are perfectly designed for what they do.

AIR MOBILITY COMMAND

Thunderbirds

The Thunderbirds are the air demonstration squadron of the air force. They tour the world's air shows performing aerobatic feats. They are the fastest flying flight demonstration team in the world.

Thunderbird pilots perform death-defying maneuvers like the one below. They must practice hard to get to this standard. There are six pilots in the team, and they spend several months practicing over the winter before the air show season starts in March.

Two F-16s demonstrate reflection passes.

In addition to being the official air force aerial demonstration team, the Thunderbirds are part of our combat force. The team and their aircraft can be made combat-ready in less than 72 hours!

A Thunderbird pilot prepares to take off for a practice sortie in her F-16 as her crew chief looks on.

SSgt Adrian

Unmanned Aircraft

An unmanned aerial vehicle (UAV), or drone, is an aircraft without a human pilot on board. Its flight is either controlled by on-board computers or by remote control on the ground.

The RQ-4 Global Hawk can fly very high, in an area known as the "edge of space." Global Hawk is an eye in the sky, providing intelligence, surveillance, and reconnaissance. It has a remote crew of three—two pilots and a sensor operator. Global Hawk pilots are all trained aircraft pilots, too. They say that during a Global Hawk flight it seems just like a flying a manned aircraft.

Global Hawk

FACT FILE

UAVs can be used for:

Target and decoys – providing a target that behaves like an enemy aircraft or missile

Reconnaissance – providing battlefield intelligence

Combat – attacking high-risk targets

Logistics – moving cargo

The Predator is an armed drone. It can find, track, fix, and fire on targets. The basic crew for the Predator is a pilot to control the aircraft and an aircrew member to operate sensors and weapons. They operate the drone remotely, from the ground. The Predator has infrared sensors, and day and night cameras. It can fire missiles and various other weapons.

A Predator drone operator

A MQ-1 Predator coming in to land.

Weather Forecasters

Accurate weather forecasts are vital for missions. The air force monitors weather conditions and how they affect Earth, the sky, and space. Combat weather teams provide weather information for flying missions local to the combat area.

Combat weather teams give pilots information on weather conditions for takeoff, landing, and in between. They monitor heat levels on personnel and advise them on how much water to drink and exercise to do. Their equipment can check wind, temperature, humidity, cloud height, and rainfall. It can even detect lightning. Teams are often dropped into a hostile area days before a mission to report on conditions.

This team is looking after the equipment at a Forward Operating Base in Iraq.

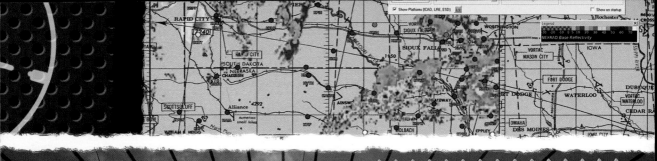

This equipment monitors the Sun. It looks for solar flares, which can disrupt communications.

FACT FILE

Weather technicians work in solar **observatories**, watching space weather. They are based all around the world so they never let the Sun slip from view. Weather specialists track typhoons in the Pacific and Indian Oceans, too. The air force also provides all the weather support for the army and is embedded in all major army units.

Operating day and night, in all climates, combat weathermen are fit and trained to use light weapons. They do some of the toughest training in the US military. Their training, as well as their unique mission, earns them the right to wear the gray beret.

Glossary

bombardment
(bom-BARD-mint)
A prolonged attack, especially with artillery or bombers.

canopy (KA-nuh-pee)
The covering over the cockpit of an aircraft.

carbon-fiber
(KAR-bun FY-ber)
A very strong lightweight synthetic fiber.

flex (FLEKS)
To bend.

g-forces (GEE-fors-ez)
The force of gravity or acceleration on a body.

infrared (in-fruh-RED)
Light outside the visible spectrum at its red end.

integrity
(in-TEH-grih-tee)
Total honesty and sincerity.

mechanic
(mih-KA-nik)
A person who works with his or her hands; especially a repairer of machines.

navigators
(NA-vuh-gay-terz)
People in charge of directing the course of a ship or aircraft.

observatories
(ub-ZUR-vuh-tor-eez)
Places or institutions equipped with instruments for observation of natural objects and events.

oxygen (OK-sih-jen)
A colorless, tasteless, odorless gas that forms about 21 percent of the atmosphere.

radar (RAY-dahr)
A device that sends out radio waves for detecting and locating an object.

reconnaissance
(ree-CON-ih-sens)
A survey (as of enemy territory) to gain information.

refuels (ree-FYOOLZ)
Provides with or takes on more fuel.

technicians (tek-NIH-shenz)
Specialists in the technical details of a subject or occupation.

WEBSITES

Due to the changing nature of Internet links, PowerKids Press has developed an online list of websites related to the subject of this book. This site is updated regularly. Please use this link to access the list:

www.powerkidslinks.com/poc/air/

Read More

Cooke, Tim. *US Airborne Forces.* Ultimate Special Forces. New York: PowerKids Press, 2013.

Jackson, Kay. *Military Planes in Action.* Amazing Military Vehicles. New York: PowerKids Press, 2009.

Zobel, Derek. *United States Air Force.* Torque Books: Armed Forces. Minneapolis, MN: Bellwether Media, 2008.

Index